Lead On, SNOOPY

Charles M. Schulz

Selected cartoons from
COULD YOU BE MORE PACIFIC?

FAWCETT CREST • NEW YORK

A Fawcett Crest Book
Published by Ballantine Books
Copyright © 1991 by United Feature Syndicate, Inc.
PEANUTS Comic Strips © 1988 by United Feature Inc.

http://www.randomhouse.com

ISBN 0-449-22023-0

This book comprises portions of COULD YOU BE MORE PACIFIC? and is reprinted by arrangement with Pharos Books.

Printed in Canada

First Ballantine Books Edition: February 1993

11 10 9 8

Lead On, SNOOPY

10-23

CHARLIE BROWN, SNOOPY, and the whole PEANUTS gang... by CHARLES M. SCHULZ